EMOTIONAL INTELLIGENCE MASTERY

A Practical 21-Day Guide to Improve
Your Relationships, Increase Your EQ
and Master Your Emotions

THOMAS SCOFIELD

THOMAS SCOFIELD

Copyright © 2018 Thomas Scofield

All rights reserved.

TABLE OF CONTENTS

Introduction

Congratulations on purchasing *Emotional Intelligence Mastery: A Practical 21-Day Guide to Improve Your Relationships, Increase Your EQ and Master Your Emotions*. We hope that this book will prove useful to you and that you will spread the word to your friends.

The following chapters will discuss everything you need to know about your EQ, or your emotional intelligence, and how you can take steps over a 21-day period to improve your emotional intelligence. It won't be easy, but we promise that it'll be worth it. If you take the time to work through each of these chapters, you will come away with greater empathy, a clearer understanding of what it takes to have a high EQ, and a heightened awareness of your own emotions.

In this technologically connected and hurried world, being able to truly connect with other people is invaluable. Whether you are the CEO looking to hone your communication skills further, or someone just wanting to learn more about making lasting and valuable connections, we are confident that everything in this book will help you accomplish those goals. We want to help people develop a part of themselves that is often ignored. EQ is often ignored for the sake of acknowledging a person's IQ: what people know about Einstein is that his IQ was in the triple digits. People like Steve Jobs and Mark

Zuckerberg are revered for their brain power, but nobody seems to really consider the emotional intelligence of these prominent figures.

It's time to broaden our understanding of how we can strive to better ourselves. Successful people often have both a high IQ and a high EQ. Your IQ, otherwise known as your potential for intelligence, is pretty much fixed. There is only so much you can do to become smarter. EQ, on the other hand, is something that can be endlessly improved upon.

This book isn't a boring essay that repeats the same abstract concepts for dozens of pages. We wanted to create something helpful and that you actually wanted to read.

You'll find 21 chapters, one for each day of your journey, and in each chapter you'll be given a task. Some tasks are simple and can be completed in one day, others are longer-term goals and will act as a compass to orient your journey and inspire you.

Make sure to try your best at completing them, and we promise that you will have a higher EQ by the time you are done reading this book. We are also confident that honing your EQ will equip you to achieve anything you set your mind to.

If you want to get the most out of this practical guide, we advise you not to read the whole book in one or two sittings. Instead, try reading a new chapter every morning after you wake up. This will provide you a clear path to follow and will help you take action to increase your EQ and master your emotions.

We strived to provide useful, actionable and to-the-point advice, so that you'll be able to finish each chapter in a couple of minutes and start taking action as soon as possible. If you're really busy or like to plan your days in advance, you can also read one chapter every night before going to bed, so that you'll already know your task for the next day.

There are plenty of books on this subject on the market, so thank you for choosing this one. Enjoy!

Day 1:
The Joy of Silence

There is so much value in silence. When the world is silent, you can hear your heart beating, the blood pulsing in your ears, the wind rushing in and out of your lungs. You can listen to what feels like an entire universe contained within one person. It is truly magical.

Once you become aware of the magic in your physical body, the magic of your mind will begin to open as well. If you were to sit still for a minute and fully pay attention to how many thoughts run through your mind within those 60 seconds, you may actually start to feel overwhelmed. The idea here though is to realize that not every thought that occurs to you has to affect you. Just watch them come and go, like you're a spectator. Don't become invested in what you're watching – just watch and observe. There is true power in not letting yourself be affected by these thoughts.

That power is invaluable yet most people never experience. This is due to the fact that the value of silence is truly the first step in mastering your emotions and increasing your emotional intelligence. The daunting task of getting to know and understand yourself begins with learning to quiet your thoughts and be comfortable within your own mind.

Here is your first task to start developing your emotional intelligence: spend an entire day in complete and utter silence. Obviously, to avoid making people upset and to avoid complication at work, you're going to need to both warn people ahead of time and communicate in other ways – email, text, etc. But, don't speak a word. Learn to keep your mouth shut and your eyes and ears open, because here's the thing: we often spend so much time talking that we rarely spend any time actually listening.

How many times do you catch yourself nodding along when someone else is talking, just to make them think you're paying attention? How often do you find your mind wandering during a work meeting or in the midst of a conversation with a loved one?

Even worse, try to think about how many times you were in a conversation where instead of truly listening to understand what the other person was saying, you were merely taking in their words so that you could formulate a response. How incredibly arrogant – to think that their words are merely a launchpad for you to build your argument.

So spend a day. Don't talk. Just listen. Develop solid listening skills and begin to think about how we could all do better to listen with more than our ears, but to listen with our hearts, and with our souls.

Day 2:
A Cup of Coffee

This chapter is all about coffee, though the coffee isn't the point here. Make it tea, make it lemonade, make it whatever beverage you like. The lesson here is to invite someone to enjoy that beverage with you.

The challenge is to refrain from falling into the comfort of inviting your best friend or someone else you already know extremely well. Instead, you are going to want to invite someone who you don't know very well. Maybe it's that quiet person in the office who you notice always looks at you after he speaks, to gauge whether you approve of what he's said. Or, maybe it's a coworker who just started, and you know that with a toddler at home, they could really use a chance to have a conversation with other adults for a change. It doesn't really matter. What you should focus on is inviting someone who is outside of your comfort zone.

This is a surefire way for you to sharpen your conversational skills. See, a conversation is something that is two-sided. When you have a conversation with someone you have known a long time, the conversation can comfortably fluctuate between discussing things familiar to the two of you and enjoying the silent pauses in conversation together. The point of this exercise is to learn to embrace the new, the uncomfortable aspects of socializing.

Being able to carry on a conversation with someone you don't know very well is going to help develop your emotional intelligence. It will force you to actually listen and to connect with another person as you learn more about them.

So find that new person in your life – heck, maybe they're even in line too to get that cup of coffee. Ask them to sit down with you and try to have a meaningful conversation with them, as naturally as possible. Find out about where they came from, what interests them, what they're going to do that day. Who knows, maybe you'll make a new friend for life. Maybe you won't – but what you do at the very least is develop and hone a skill which will serve you well for years to come.

Day 3:
Mindfulness Meditation

This chapter is all about learning how to meditate. Meditation will make it easier for you to cut out all the mental clutter that builds up over time and get to the heart of what it is you really feel. It will also provide you with a wealth of other benefits.

While it has been a part of the Buddhist faith for more than two thousand years, mindfulness meditation has become exceedingly popular in the Western world over the past several decades thanks to its proven ability to improve mental health including the treatment of stress, anxiety and even drug addiction. Professor Jon Kabat-Zinn brought the process to the attention of the modern world in the 1970s by publishing findings that linked it to stress reduction. This, in turn, lead to a flurry of new interest in the practice and a new understanding of the myriad of different ways that being mindful can help improve one's health by directly combating numerous different ailments. Studies on the topic have even proven so conclusive that it is now common to see mindfulness meditation being practiced everywhere from hospitals to prisons to veteran associations.

Since its inception, mindfulness meditation been proven via scientific study to improve the physical wellbeing of those that practice it on a regular basis. At its heart, mindfulness meditation is all about focusing your mind to ensure that you are as fully aware of each moment as fully as possible. This, in turn, allows you to exist more completely in any given moment by expanding your consciousness to the fullest.

While it might sound like a tall order at first, the truth of the matter is that being mindful is a skill which means it can be improved by regular practice in much the same way as any other skill. Luckily, practicing mindfulness meditation is as easy as finding a few moments to focus solely on the present and the information that your senses are providing you at the moment. In fact, if you can find just fifteen minutes a day to practice, you will soon find that your overall stress is likely to decrease and your sense of self is likely to be at an all-time high. This isn't just an ephemeral feeling either, neuroimaging performed on those who practice mindfulness meditation on a regular basis shows that their minds actually process information more effectively, they are able to more easily regulate their emotions and their attention spans than those who do not make the practice a part of their daily routine.

While one of the best things about mindfulness meditation is its malleable nature, when you are first getting started it is recommended that you set some time aside each day to specifically devote to the practice. Ideally, this means someplace quiet and during a time of day when you already feel relaxed so that there is nothing stopping you from devoting up to 30 minutes to the exercise. Remember, being mindful is all about creating space between the sensory information your body is providing your mind, as well as the way you process the information that does make it through. As such, the fewer stimuli that you have to actively deal with, the easier you will find the entire practice to be.

As with any new habit, it is crucial that you create a routine around your mindfulness meditation practices for the best results. Generally speaking, you can expect it to take about 30 days for a new habit to really stick which means that you will need to commit to going hard for just four weeks before you can expect to start seeing the best results.

Unfortunately, due to its few requirements and low impact nature, it is often quite easy to push off your set mindfulness meditation time for a later than never comes, especially if they are already very busy as it stands. If you find yourself always coming up with an excuse to get out of meditating at the moment, you may find the following piece of advice particularly useful. "Practice mindfulness meditation for fifteen minutes every day unless, of course, you are extremely busy in which case you should practice for thirty minutes instead." Don't let the outside world intrude on your potential for inner peace, find a time each day that works for you and stick with it no matter what; in a month's time, you will be glad you did.

In order to get started successfully, the first thing you are going to need to do is to find yourself someplace quiet and secluded where you won't be interrupted. With practice, you will be able to reliably practice mindfulness virtually anywhere, but for now, you will want all the help you can get. The end goal with mindfulness meditation is to quiet the mind as a means of finding an internal calm regardless of what might be going on in the outside world.

It is difficult for many people to reach that state right out of the gate, however, which is why many people find a great way to get to be putting all of your effort in to taking in all of the information your senses are providing you with at once. Your senses are always providing you with a constant stream of sensory data that your brain, by and large, filters out. With mindfulness meditation, you make a conscious choice to let all of that information in, starting with deep breaths.

You are going to want to start by breathing in fully, using your diaphragm, until your lungs are completely full. As you do so, feel your lungs expand as the air enters them, consider the temperature of the air and the smells that it brings along with it. As you breathe out, feel your lungs contract and feel the way the air flows out of your body.

From there, let your senses expand outward and take in everything that is going on around you. When taking in the information around you, it is important to make a conscious effort not to judge the information that you are taking in, only to experience it. Judging the things that you are experiencing can easily lead to additional related thoughts or a comparison of multiple different situations, and by then your mind will be running a mile a minute as normal.

If one of your thoughts catches your attention more directly, all you need to do is take a mental step back from it and let it go. Giving the thought any more time, even if it is just to chastise yourself for your shortcomings, is only interacting with the thought even more and won't lead to anything productive. Once you reach a point where your thoughts have died down and you are existing as fully at the moment as possible, the last step is to simply remain in this state for as long as possible. With practice, you will find that this exercise helps you purge negative thoughts from your mind as well.

What's more, given enough practice you may even find that you are able to maintain a state of mindfulness even when you are largely focused on the world around you. Being mindful means always being connected to a soothing, calming, mental state along with one that is full of peace and joy which benefits not just you but everyone around you.

Day 4:

Pay it Forward and Backward

Hopefully the idea of "paying it forward" is not going to be a revolutionary concept to you. The basics are simple, oftentimes, once you've extended your hand and raised someone else to a new level, they'll be in a position to do that for someone else too. You cannot become successful and you cannot become emotionally intelligent until you begin to care for other people. Once you realize that you have the ability to help others and start doing so, you will be amazed at how much your life will change. Your relationships with people will become so much easier to both begin and maintain.

Like attracts like. When you begin to live like you have abundance and like you are able to help people, you will attract people who live in abundance and who like to help people. But learning to live like that doesn't happen overnight. You need to start building habits in your life that will deepen your emotional intelligence and will make you a better person overall.

That is the action part of this chapter: go out today and share a small act of kindness. Buy someone's groceries, someone's cup of coffee, or someone's tank of gas. Whatever it is you can afford, go and take care of it for someone else. And be sneaky about it – this is not about trying to garner praise and admiration. It's about putting that good energy out into the universe and trusting that it will come back to you in spades.

It's about learning how to be selfless. Yes, we live in an age where we preach self-care and self-love, both of which are incredibly important! However, no man (or woman) is an island - we are all connected. When you contribute toward one person's good fortune, you are indirectly contributing toward your own. As each person's fortunes are raised, they, in turn, have the opportunity to pass that forward. Hurricanes are started by butterfly wings, right? Start your own hurricane of human kindness. Flood the world with some love, and trust that your actions will make a difference.

A note on anonymity: Sometimes the anonymity of small acts of kindness can make us feel like we really aren't doing anything much when we chip in five bucks to the homeless man on the corner or donate our spare change at the cash register to St. Jude's. This might dissuade you from continuing to do these small acts, but it's important to remember that a dessert is made up of millions of tiny grains of sand. Without your contribution, no matter how small and insignificant you may think it is, things would not get done. Plus, that five dollars may have been the difference between that homeless person getting a meal that day, or experiencing further starvation. That spare change contributes to keeping the lights on at St. Jude's.

The people who benefit from your generosity may not know your name or how much you donated. Regardless, you made a difference in someone's life. That's the important part here. Make the donation, pay for someone's coffee. Be the reason why someone smiles today. Your recognition doesn't matter, but their smile does. Your reward is the boost to your EQ that you received as a result of breaking out of your traditional mindset and focusing exclusively on others.

Day 5:
Improve Your Ability to Express Yourself

This chapter is all about learning how to express yourself. While this expression should never make others feel bad or be done in a way that harms another person, it is still important to spend some time expressing yourself and letting others know how you feel. Emotional intelligence is not just about listening and understanding how others are, it is also about being able to effectively express your own thoughts, emotions, and feelings as well and this is one part that some people will struggle with. Let's take a look at some of the things that you can do to better express yourself.

It really does not matter what others think about you. In this society, it is hard to remember this, but in reality, the only person whose opinion should matter to you is your own. We are so used to hearing how we have to fit in and how we should want everyone to like us, but this is just not a reality in most cases. No matter how hard you work, some people are going to talk, some will get angry, and some are going to laugh and even make fun of you. The good news is, most people aren't doing any of these things, so even if you make a mistake, it is not as big of a deal as you may think.

We spend way too much time trying to impress those who are around us. We want to be liked, we want others to always think highly of us. We get to the point where if we make even a little mistake, we assume that everyone saw it and is making fun of us. But this is not reality. Most people aren't paying that much attention and even out of the ones who notice, most don't really think it is that big of a deal. We can make mountains out of mole hills all we want, but most people are too busy with what is going on in their own lives to always watch what is going on in yours.

This should be liberating to you. Spending all that time worrying about what others think about you is exhausting and can put anyone on edge. Instead of focusing on what others think about you, it is time to focus on what you think about yourself. From now on, when you do an activity of any sort, don't think about how your coworkers or friends will react, think about how you will feel when the action is done.

As long as you believe you can stand behind your actions after the fact, regardless of what others might think about them, them go ahead and move forward, you really have very little to lose. However, if you feel the action you are considering might leave you feeling ashamed of what you are doing, then you may be better off just picking another course instead. With everything that you do in life, concentrate on impressing yourself, and you will honestly start impressing other people in the process.

How many people do you know that always seem to be a little bit lost or confused? They always go along with whatever the crowd wants to do and never really gives a concrete thought or opinion of their own. They may appear happy on the surface, but underneath they likely feel resentful as they are unable to speak up for themselves, even when it is very important they do so. This resent often leads to a me against the world mentality that can be extremely harmful when it comes to improving your emotional intelligence.

If you are one of those people who always tend to follow the crowd, then odds are you need to learn to stand for something. The line you draw in the sand doesn't need to be major, it just needs to be something that you legitimately care about. For example, if you are with a group of friends who are considering where they want to go for dinner, if you don't like Thai food, and someone suggests Thai food, speak up for yourself and register your displeasure. It is unlikely that anyone is going to get offended by your announcement; on the contrary, they will take your statement into consideration and you may not have to suffer through an hour at a place that has nothing you want to eat.

This is a relatively innocuous example that, when practiced regularly, will make it far easier to get into the habit of speaking up for yourself than you otherwise might. In fact, much of the frustration that comes along with modern life actually occurs because people are too worried about angering those around them which causes them to remain quiet to their own detriment. But when you live your life always worrying about what others think and never getting to do what you want, it can make you stressed and angry and you will likely lose that emotional intelligence because you won't be able to see things from the other point of view.

Of course, your stance should never be cruel and it should take others into consideration. You still need to think about what others like and be empathetic for them, but this doesn't mean that you need to be run over all the time either.

While having people respect you certainly beats the alternative, it is important to remember that it is hardly the end of the world if they don't. While this is the opposite of what the digital world teaches, it really is true, the only person you need to worry about impressing is yourself. Regardless of how hard you might work, there are always going to be some people that talk behind your back or get angry when you succeed. If you live your life to the fullest, however, then it is likely to be a small fraction of the whole that you won't need to think twice about which means it is much less of a big deal than it may appear to be at the time.

In order to express yourself to the fullest, the first thing you will want to be aware of is that, regardless of how important or embarrassing something might seem to you at the moment, a vast majority of people will have forgotten about it completely forgotten about it by the next day or, what's even more likely, not even register it in the first place.

It is important to keep this in mind as one of the difficult parts of self-expression that many people fail to master is getting past the thought that other people are going to judge them for expressing themselves in an unguarded way. The truth of the matter is often the complete opposite, most people tend to be so wrapped up in their own personal drama that they won't think twice about anything you say or do, good or bad, which means they will never think anything is nearly as big of a deal as you do.

Day 6:
Write it Out

Writing out your feelings can definitely help make you a more emotionally intelligent human. It's not that the act of starting a journal or writing will automatically make you a more self-aware, more empathetic person. This particular exercise is going to be targeted. This is not meant to be an exercise in teaching you how to keep a journal – there is a different purpose here.

The purpose in keeping this particular journal is for you to keep track of your emotions. Start keeping track of when you feel extreme emotions. Write down when you feel angry, when you feel euphoric when you feel like you just might rattle out of your skin because you are so nervous. I want you to write down the times when you feel emotions that are extreme.

Let's start with anger. Begin writing when you feel angry. When your teeth start to grind and your fists begin to clench – grab a pen and start writing. Don't start talking or arguing or doing anything rash. Write down exactly what you are feeling. Write out what happened, from start to finish. Record what triggered you and got you feeling this way.

Then, as you calm down, write about what you were feeling as you calmed down. Write about what helped you to calm down. I want you to pay attention to the transition in your feelings. Figure out what made you so angry – was it a particular gesture or maybe a way something was said? By essentially writing out all of your emotions, you start to become more in touch with them. By becoming more in touch with your own emotions, you heighten your emotional intelligence.

But this doesn't have to just be about anger. You can also journal about your experiences with euphoria. Who doesn't like to figure out what makes them happy? When you start to feel happy, do the same thing that you do when you write about being angry. Start at the beginning. What caused you to start feeling happy? Was it a word, was it an event that happened? Maybe it was a person. Figure that out and write it down. Essentially you are acting like your own therapist.

Think through these emotions and figure out what makes you tick. Now, how will this help you become a more emotionally intelligent human? Think of it this way: when you run into someone who is extremely angry, wouldn't it be helpful to see if you could calm him or her down? Don't you think you could help the situation instead of making it worse?

When we begin to understand our own emotions and figure out what makes us tick, we can then better understand what makes other people tick. While each person's emotional makeup is about as different as their genetic makeup, certain emotions and reactions are the same across humanity. When we can identify a similar emotion in another human being and then react with empathy and kindness instead of misunderstanding and hurt, we can make our interactions with one another so much better.

Day 7:
My Dinner With…Me?

The point of this chapter is to talk to you about how to use taking yourself to dinner as a way to deepen your emotional intelligence. What happens when we go to dinner? We order food, we interact with the wait staff, and we try to enjoy ourselves. It is the point in our day when we truly let go of ourselves and relax.

Part of the reason why you should take yourself out to dinner is that it is a chance to let your guard down around yourself. It is a chance for you to experience all of your emotions without having to put up a front or having to fake any kind of emotion because other people are there with you. It is a chance for you to get to know yourself better.

How often do we really take the time to get to know ourselves and understand our own feelings? The answer? Not very often. We spend so much time trying to read everyone else around us and trying to figure out how we need to respond in that exact moment, that we never take a second to analyze what is going on within ourselves.

Because we fail to take the time to understand ourselves, we do ourselves a great disservice. When we fail to take the time to understand ourselves, we are not allowing ourselves to deepen our emotional intelligence. Your emotional intelligence depends upon figuring out your own internal cues and your own internal emotional reactions to things. When we understand ourselves, we are better able to take a moment and not react instinctively to people who upset us.

It also gives us a chance to reflect on other people. When we reflect on other people, we give ourselves a chance to understand where they are coming from. When we understand where people are coming from, we are better able to respond in a way that will help them. This is the essence of having and using emotional intelligence. We are trying to go through life in a way that allows us to interact positively with people. We can interact positively with people when we understand why they are reacting to a situation in a certain way.

When we begin to understand our own emotions as adults, we can better respond to other adults and their tantrums too. Because believe me when I say, adults throw their share of tantrums too. But when we take ourselves out to dinner and we are able to truly connect with our flow of consciousness, we can get a clear view of how our emotions flow through us.

When we take ourselves out to dinner, we also have the chance to learn how to respect other people's' flow of your emotional consciousness. When we understand that other people also let down their guard at certain times and break down the wall which holds back their flow of emotions, then we can be more accepting when that happens in real life. Ultimately, when we are more accepting, we are more emotionally intelligent.

Day 8:
Become More Confident

Building your self-confidence is a dream that many people have but that few people actually follow through on. This is because it can be very difficult to get started if you don't already have plenty of self-confidence, to begin with. Self-confidence is also important when it comes to expressing yourself and your EQ in either the short or the long-term. Even if your self-confidence is in the dumps there are still a number of useful exercises you can do in order to force your mind to see things in a self-confident way.

If you find yourself becoming afraid when it is time to be confident, it is important to understand that the only way to really face this particular fear once and for all is if you master it completely. If you aren't sure about the outcome of a specific event, this uncertainty can easily turn into anticipation which can then turn into fear if you aren't careful. Reacting with anxiety at a time when you should be reacting with self-confidence will destroy any momentum that you may have built up in the interim which means you will end up back at square one.

Thinking about all the ways that being more self-confident will help you in the future may take your mind off the present, but it won't do much to get you started when it comes to improving your day-to-day interactions with others. At some point, you need to put your new and improved thoughts into actions.

While stretching your comfort zone will be difficult at first, the fact that it is just as difficult for everyone else to do the same should make those first few steps easier. While it may be hard to believe, the only real difference between you and those with the self-confidence that you admire is that when confronted with their initial obstacles, they overcame. All you need to do is follow their example.

If you can't convince yourself that you aren't going to fail, do yourself a favor and stop focusing on it. If you instead take the idea that you are going to fail as a fact, you can stop dreading it so much and instead think of everything that follows as an opportunity for learning. If you learn as much as you can about the situation in question, then you improve your odds of doing things better the next time. What's more, without the added pressure of worrying about failing, you may just find that you exceed your own expectations.

While this may be easier said than done, understanding that everyone is the center of their own universe can make the idea of trying and failing much easier to handle. Just keep telling yourself that what feels like major, embarrassing events to you, may very well be completely glossed over by those around you. Failure by itself is nothing to be ashamed of, trying and failing once may even make trying a second time that much easier.

Many people who feel as though they lack self-confidence find themselves with a growing fit of fright whenever they perceive an incident incoming that would be handled more deftly by those who are already self-confident. This is a reductive mentality, however, and one that you will need to put aside in favor of seeing the oncoming experience as a time for learning, rather than fright. This can be easier said than done, however, though one or more of the following suggestions on how to go about doing so may work for you.

The next time you feel a bout of fright or anxiety coming on, in a situation where you believe being self-confident would improve your response, you may be able to spin it to yourself as a form of curiosity instead. Specifically, if you think of what is to come as a learning experience on the road to improving your overall level of self-confidence then you may find that anxiety is replaced with curiosity, allowing things to move forward more smoothly than they otherwise might.

If cognitive refraining doesn't work, the next thing you may want to try is taking a moment to ask what it is exactly that you are afraid of. While the answer might seem obvious at first, with a little bit of rational consideration you may be surprised at how different the reality of the worst thing that can happen is when compared with the nameless dread that was building in your stomach. With the truth of the matter on the table, you will be surprised at how much easier it is to move forward, increasing your self-confidence in the process.

In the moments where you are having an extremely hard time getting over the hump of your own insecurities and projecting confidence to the fullest degree possible, instead of wallowing in doubt, consider using these moments as a powerful catalyst for change. What could be more different at the moment than acting confident instead of worrying about what you lack? From there, that success will make it easier for a repeat performance and so on and so forth.

While understanding where your fear related to instances which typically require self-confidence comes from is useful, it is important that you don't get so caught up in self-analysis that you ultimately forget to act. Those who are self-confident know that there is a time to plan and a time to act confidently on the plan that they created if you are trying to do the same then you will want to ensure that you are working towards success with both parts of the equation.

Once you start to approach life in a more confident fashion, it will naturally assert itself as part of your day to day interactions. While this is certainly an understandable extension of all of the work you are doing, it is important to not overdo it by taking advantage of those who have not yet learned that confidence is merely a state of mind. Specifically, it is important to be seen as being assertive, without crossing over the line into actively being aggressive which is why you will want to be aware of the verbal and physical expressions you use when speaking your mind to ensure you properly walk the line between confidence and arrogance. Be mindful of the ways in which you assert yourself by keeping the following tips in mind the next time you head out into the world.

While you are still working on establishing a baseline level of self-confidence in social situations one of the best ways to go about doing so is by making a habit of sticking up for yourself when you feel as though you are getting the short end of the stick. If you don't stand up for yourself when the opportunity arises then you are essentially giving anyone that witnesses the initial incident a free pass to walk all over you as you are not important enough to warrant an extension of basic respect.

What's worse, this will only reinforce the types of negative habits that you are no doubt working so very hard to change. Specifically, things like changing yourself for others and seeking external approval instead of working to be happy with yourself and who you are personally are both common traps that those without self-confidence fall into.

Day 9:
My Dinner With…My Mom?

First, you probably owe your mom more dinners than you will ever be able to buy her. Let's face facts, she has been feeding since you took your first breath, and you probably have only bought her dinner once or twice. Considering she is the person who literally gave you life, it seems appropriate that you go ahead and buy her dinner. So the first lesson of this chapter is that you need to treat your mother with respect, and that includes buying her dinner.

In this chapter, we are going to focus on how we can effectively communicate with another person and find out more about them. Because while it is useful to fully understand our own emotions, that is only half the battle of obtaining emotional intelligence. In order to truly develop your emotional intelligence, we must develop skills in terms of how we communicate with other people and how we are able to make them feel cared for and loved.

This is why it makes sense to start with your mother. When you call to set up this date with your mother, make sure that you ask her where she wants to go for dinner. Let her know that this evening is all about her. If she has a favorite restaurant that you absolutely despise, suck it up for one evening and go eat dinner there. While you are sucking it up, keep that emotion to yourself. This evening is about her. It's not usually a good idea to quash your own emotions, but sometimes for the greater good, it is necessary. Here, the greater good is making your mother feel like she is not imposing on you.

While you're at dinner, talk with her about her hopes and dreams. Talk with her about what she wanted when she was a little girl. See if you can get her to talk about what she wanted to be when she grew up and the steps that she took to become that person. See if you can get her to talk about your childhood and what she did to make sure that you had the best life that she could give you. Listen with more than just your ears. Listen with your whole heart and your whole soul. See if you can get a read on her emotions from her voice. Close your eyes if you have to, but really pay attention to the emotions behind her words.

Talk about how she gave up some of her dreams and some of her wants when she was raising you. She's probably not going to want to talk about this but it is important that you understand that sacrifices were made for you to have the life that you have now. It is important for you to understand this, because we so often take things in our life, like our mothers, for granted. If you can get a sense of the sacrifices that she may for you when you were young, then you will start to see your mother is more than just your mother. You will begin to see her as a person. As she develops into a whole new person before your eyes, you will start to get a better feeling for who she is as a person, not just who she is as a mother.

Because she was not always just mom. She gave up a lot of her life to make sure that you're happy. This because your mother is your best chance to truly understand how love and sacrifice are intertwined.

Those two things go together like bread and butter. When we love someone, truly love someone, we give things up for that person. When we understand that love and sacrifice are connected, we start to develop new levels of emotional intelligence.

When we understand that in order to give our kid that quality education, we may need to forego that new car, we are being emotionally intelligent. When we give that toddler who refuses to eat their own meal some food off of our own plate, we become more emotionally intelligent.

Becoming emotionally intelligent is understanding that there is give and take in our emotions. It is understanding that the world does not just revolve around our wants and needs. We share this planet with other human beings and that means that we cannot always get what we want. But when you are learning to become emotionally intelligent, this fact does not upset you. Instead, you welcome the idea that there is give and take in this life. You welcome it because you know that in order for this planet to keep spinning, we all need to work together. In order to work together, we need to be emotionally intelligent.

Day 10:
Adoption

When we learn to care for another living thing, we learn to put someone else's needs ahead of our own. This is important in learning emotional intelligence because as we have spoken about before, if you do not understand that we are all connected in this world and that our emotions have give-and-take, then you will never truly develop emotional intelligence. Emotional intelligence is about not just understanding your own emotions but understanding and being able to respond to other emotions and other people as well.

A simple way to start learning that is to just buy a plant. If you haven't ever given it much thought, you will be surprised at how needy some plants can be. Some plants need full sunlight and a special type of fertilizer while others require watering only during a full moon every third Tuesday. Perhaps you have already learned how to keep a plant alive. If you have, congratulations! You can now move on to the next step. Go adopt a creature. Learn about what it takes to make them thrive and make sure you do everything in your power to make that happen. Go talk to your vet, go take in an obedience class with your new pet at a pet store, do whatever it takes for your particular creature to thrive and do that. Your entire lifestyle may have to change.

This means that your next vacation may either need to be put on hold or that you will somehow have to find a person that you trust enough to go into your home and take care of your pets. This is going to take some effort on your part as you consider what another living being needs. This will teach you that in order to take care of something that is another sentient being, you will need to consider how your life impacts theirs. If you were not able to go home every few hours to water your plants, your plants would not care. But your dog or your cat would very much care. At the end of the day, this is about learning how to put someone else's needs above your own.

Emotionally intelligent people are able to understand that sometimes they need to put their own needs on hold in order to make sure that someone else or something else has what it needs to survive and thrive. So if you want to increase your emotional intelligence, you will need to learn this skill. The best way to learn this skill is to introduce another living being into your life and then take care of it.

Day 11:
Take a Look at How You Interact with Others

Relationship management is the analysis, identification and of course management of relationships with people who are inside and outside your social circle as well as the development through coaching and feedback. It incorporates your ability to persuade, communicate and lead all the while remaining direct and honest.

If you hope to successfully manage relationships, then you need to use what you have learned to far in order to determine how you and the other party are affecting one another and what effect external forces are having on the scenario you now find yourself dealing with. Only by having a clear and accurate picture of all the moving pieces will you be able to find the right solution to please everyone.

Your first clue of how a conversation is going is to monitor what it is your partner is saying, as well as how they are saying it. For example, if you are talking about the weather with a complete stranger in an elevator, you can determine a lot from such a short interaction. Is the person engaged with the conversation, or just responding simply to your remarks? If a person answers your questions with a simple yes or no, they are likely not interested in furthering the conversation. The interpretation of why is a layer deeper, which you may not have the opportunity to explore.

Active listening is very important in effective communication, as well as in building a good relationship with someone new. Now, everybody already knows that you should learn to listen, however, only a few people actually know how to listen properly. What you need to learn is active listening in which you make the other person feel as though you are not just listening to what they are saying but that you are engaged by it. This is an excellent technique for building a good rapport with the other person. Whether you have social anxiety or not, this is definitely a technique that is a must for you to learn. So, how do you perform active listening? There are certain guidelines that you need to know:

You should learn to use follow-up questions. For example, if a person tells you that they are feeling sad, ask why they are feeling that way. This helps to show that you are interested in what they are saying. While this is an admittedly basic example, it still serves to show the other person that you are interested while also allowing them to open up about whatever it is they are talking about at the same time.

Make sure that you respond accordingly. A person can easily tell if you are listening to them by the way you respond. Keeping your responses relative to the topic should be easy, as long as you truly listen to what the other person is telling you.

By repeating what the other person is telling you, it tells them that you are able to follow their train of thought. This is usually paired with a follow-up question. For example, if a person tells you that they went to the beach, you can say, "Oh, you went to the beach? When?" As you can see, you do not really add anything new. You simply guide and help the other person to express themselves.

Ironically, a good way to begin changing how you interpret someone else's emotions is by disconnecting from them a bit. For example, you may interpret a friend blowing you off as personally offensive, just as most people would. Instead of letting your own feelings spiral into anger and questions about your self-worth, you need to disconnect and try and find a logical solution to the events that have arisen. Maybe this person is stuck in traffic, and their phone is dead. Maybe they had an emergency and could not contact you to reschedule your rendezvous.

Giving people the benefit of the doubt and assuming that they have the best intentions is good practice. Be positive and always try to consider both sides of a situation before reacting negatively. If someone cuts you off in traffic, think about how they might be late for work, and if they are late again, they might be fired. They need that spot in line more than you do. Most importantly, people make mistakes and sometimes you just need to let it go.

Knowing how someone else is feeling is always a complicated matter. In essence, you can never really know how someone is feeling because their emotions are their own. You do not have the same life knowledge that they do, therefore your perspective of any given situation will likely not be the same. Instead of insisting that you can see it from their angle, try creating an open dialogue in which they can express those feelings so that you may better comprehend them.

This doesn't mean having a deep-rooted therapy session every time a conflict arises, but simply asking for a person's thoughts before drawing your own conclusions is good practice. Start the conversation with verbiage like "How would you feel if..." or "Would it be too bold to ask...". This gives the person the opportunity to speak up for themselves, an opportunity that simply demanding or stating a fact does not present.

If you are struggling with the whole idea of empathy, it may be time to start working on it a bit more. Start with one person. Make it your goal for the week to think the way that this particular person would in each situation. Instead of acting the way that you would or think that you would react the way that you think they would. This can help you to get a deeper understanding of what is going on with those around you.

Day 12:
Biting Your Tongue

If you have a partner, then this chapter might seem pretty dramatic. The goal here is to go and spend the day doing everything that they want to do. If they want to just nap in the sun, then get cozy. If they want to talk about their hopes and dreams and tell you about the novel idea that they have but have never actually written, then you need to sit there and listen. Take the cheesy pictures and go to the crazy cat conventions.

Just let them have their day. As long as you aren't going all Daredevil and deciding to be a vigilante or going on a giant crime spree, just indulge your partner. If you are with this person, you clearly have some sort of feelings for them. Even if they are not particularly romantic feelings because it is early in the relationship, just give it a try. Even if you don't stay together or you don't end up catching feelings, it is still an important experience to allow another person to have a day that is all about them and just support them through it.

Now here's the catch: you can't be sour about it. You have to make a genuine effort to be happy and supportive. You cannot make snide comments and instead must make every possible effort to keep your partner smiling the entire day. Don't make them feel like they are imposing on you or that they are being selfish. Make sure they understand that you are a willing participant here. This will make them enjoy the day without any guilt, which is kind of the whole point.

You just might enjoy yourself and see things from another person's perspective. After all, emotional intelligence is about being able to see things from another person's point of view. The takeaway here: make someone else feel good and learn to see something new from a different perspective.

Day 13:
Get Out of Your Comfort Zone

The goal of this chapter is to tell you to go take a hike! Seriously. Go. Get out of here. Go commune with nature for a little bit. If that is already something that is in your wheelhouse, then go take a cooking class, learn how to ice skate, learn how to rock climb the specifics don't matter, just go learn something new. Learning something new will expose you to so much more than just the shiny new skill that you acquire. See, when you go and you learn something new, you generally have to go to a new place, meet new people, and make yourself vulnerable to failure.

Those are seriously so many opportunities for growth here: first you have to go to the new place. This means that you have to put a new location in your GPS and you have to actually drive to this new place and figure out where you are and how to get comfortable and situated. You also get to meet new people when you try new things. This means that you'll be introduced to a whole host of other experiences and other perspectives just by virtue of going and trying something new. You are meeting people who have the potential to enrich your life and teach you something that you have either always wanted to learn or something that is vital for you to learn just because it's going to push you out of your comfort zone. Everything that you want to be in life is just outside of your comfort zone. This is not just a motivational saying for a poster or a meme. This is a real life lesson.

The most valuable part of trying new things is making yourself more vulnerable to failure. Becoming vulnerable to failure is a valuable experience when you are trying to build emotional intelligence. When we fail, we learn so much more about ourselves than we do when we succeed. This is because when we fail we learn that there are opportunities for us to improve and learn new skills. Also, when we fail we learn that we are not perfect. While most people do not walk around under the assumption that they are perfect, arrogance can get the best of everyone now and again.

See, when you fail you learn about all the different gaps in your knowledge and it gives you the opportunity to fill those gaps in. When you learn that you can fill those gaps in, you expose yourself to so many different new lessons and experiences. When we were children, we fell many more times before we learned to walk. When we are learning to walk, we do not pause and think that perhaps we should give up because it is too difficult. Instead, we gathered our courage and took those next few shaky steps until we gained our sure footing and walked.

As we age, we occasionally lose sight of this initial courage that we were all born with. You forget that it is a natural part of life to fail and that failure never held us back when we were too little to understand what failure was. Understanding what failure is should not hold us back from trying new things; rather, it should inspire us to know that when we were even too young to comprehend what we were doing we were conquering our fears every single day. Now that we are old enough to recognize what it means to overcome our fears, we should be excited to do that every single day.

Whatever skill it is, make it something outside of your comfort zone. If you already know how to cook do not go take a cooking class. If you already know how to rock climb, then taking a beginners course in bouldering is not going to help you. What I want you to do is search for something that scares you. If it does not scare you it will not help you grow. The idea here is that you need to become comfortable with being uncomfortable. When we become comfortable with being uncomfortable we allow ourselves to grow.

Give yourself a little credit. After all, you have gotten this far in life. It seems only natural, that you can go a little farther if you just push yourself.

Day 14:
Tripping Forward

In this chapter, we are going to focus on traveling and how it can help you build your emotional intelligence.   Traveling can be a complicated business. Not only do you have to figure out if you can even afford to take a trip, but then you also need to figure out every bit of planning that is involved. This means that you need to search for plane tickets, make sure that you're getting a good deal on those plane tickets, and make sure that you are going to be riding on a plane that isn't just going to crash over the Atlantic.

When you are going to get on a plane, you need to take so many different things into consideration. Are you going to check your bag?

Will you just have a carry-on? Or maybe you can just shove everything into that one personal item you get and call it a day. You also need to make sure that you have accommodations set up for wherever you are going. You need to make sure that you are able to get from the airport to your accommodations and then make sure that you can travel freely around your destination.

If you are unfamiliar with your destination, this may mean hiring lots of cabs or making sure that your GPS is able to work internationally without bankrupting you. Then you need to consider the food situation. Are you in a place where you feel safe eating food from street vendors? What about the water? Can you trust the water that comes from the tap? Or are you in a place where you can't even get ice in your drink because it might make you sick?

You also need to consider what exactly you are going to pack! Do you need formal clothes? Do you need more than five outfits? Is it warm? Cold? Mild? Will it rain? Do you need an umbrella? It can be so incredibly overwhelming to travel that it is a miracle that most of us even leave our houses in the morning. And yet, millions of people travel internationally every year.

Why do they do this? Because travel will enrich your life and make you more emotionally intelligent. How? Well, let me explain. When you travel, you are exposing yourself to failure, which I have talked about at length as one of my favorite ways for you to deepen your emotional intelligence. When you are able to fail, you can learn! You can learn from your travel mistakes, so long as they are the kind that you can bounce back from.

Travel also allows you to see different people and different places. When you do this you expose yourself to new people and new cultures. This means that you are able to bridge the gap between your own experience on this earth and theirs. When that happens you are able to find common ground. Remember that? We have talked about that many, many times. Common ground will enable you to communicate so much better with people and enable you to get more unique perspectives on the world that are not your own.

If you can afford to, take a trip to a foreign country where you don't speak the language. This will help you realize that we are all dependent on one another and that the way we communicate is important. It will also help you realize that we are often all at the mercy of strangers.

Why is it important to realize that we are often at the mercy of strangers? When we understand how interconnected we all are it helps us to understand that our actions do not affect just us but they affect people that we may not even know. This causes us to be more self-reflective in our actions which means that when we are going to act, we think before we do so. Whether we like it or not, the way someone else acts can, and often does, affect our lives. Think of it this way: let's say you're driving down the street minding your own business and driving very well. All of a sudden, a drunk driver comes barreling down the road the wrong way and hits you head-on. Now, you are in the hospital dealing with injuries that you suffered because of another person's poor choices.

It was also the choice of the person who was serving them drinks, who saw they were drunk but continued to serve them drinks. It was the choice of their friends to let them drive even though they were clearly intoxicated. All of our choices, when they are made, affect people. When we are emotionally intelligent enough to understand this, then we are more circumspect in our actions and we are able to put more thought into our actions. We do not act as irresponsibly or irrationally. We are able to calmly and logically react to situations without harming other people.

Day 15:
Feedback

We all experience getting feedback at work. Sometimes it is good feedback and sometimes it isn't. But feedback, no matter whether it is positive or negative, is always valuable.

The emotionally intelligent person is able to observe the feedback without getting emotionally involved. They allow themselves to just watch and see the words without letting it affect their inner calm. This takes years of practice, obviously, and it takes a lot of effort. Nobody is just born indifferent. We all care what other people think of us, particularly when those people are paying us.

This does not mean that you will instantly be able to be impervious to any kind of emotional reaction when you get negative feedback. All you need to do is to strive for that. Try to be as impartial as possible when it comes to your own work. Understand that when people critique your work, it is not a personal attack on you. When your boss says that something could be done a different way, this is not actually code for "you are stupid and you should never come back here. "

People are there to get work done, not to put you under a microscope because it is fun for them. That is simply insane. To prove you will want to psych yourself up and then go up to your boss and have them critique a recent project that you completed for them. Have them give you the good, the bad, the ugly, all of it.

Ask for honest feedback about a project you've completed. When you receive any kind of negative feedback, write it down. This hearkens back to the journaling concept. Write about how you feel. Write about how the words they used made you feel and see if you can figure out why their word choices made you feel a certain way. Maybe you don't like it when people tell you feedback that is vague.

Contemplate it for a while and think about how it makes you feel. Make an appointment and talk with whoever gave you the feedback. Have an open and honest discussion about the criticism and most importantly – do not interrupt them. Just listen. That is going to be difficult, but do your best to only interrupt when you want to ask a clarifying question. Otherwise, just sit back and let the words wash over you.

When you have listened to that feedback and you have processed it, the next step is to come up with a plan to address whatever negativity they brought up. Make it a positive plan. This exercise will again help you put yourself in an opposing viewpoint and be able to better respond to feedback that does not necessarily jive with your own worldview.

Day 16:
Check Your Focus

What you choose to focus on is one of the most critical elements to being able to manage your emotions effectively. Whatever emotion you are focusing on at the time, you are actually feeding it, making it more powerful, and giving it enduring strength. By focusing on the negative feelings in your life, you not only strengthen them, but you weaken the positives. What you feed becomes stronger; what you starve gets weaker. Your emotions are rarely stagnating; they are either growing stronger or becoming weaker. The main part of the word "emotion" is "motion."

Your body feels the emotion before your mind comprehends its intensity or purpose. To prove my point, try a little experiment. Turn the corners of your mouth in a smile and begin to chuckle. Now strengthen that chuckle into full-blown laughter. It won't take long before your mind begins remembering something that gave you a giggle, and in just a matter of minutes, the positive is set into motion. Admit it; you weren't necessarily thinking about a happy moment before you began to laugh, right? As you focused on the real laughter, your thoughts followed with a happy memory.

The same can be said for clapping your hands and singing a happy tune. There's something about clapping your hands that won't allow you to feel depressed. Focus on the motion of clapping and the happy words to the song, and soon your outlook will be happy. It's like putting the positive in motion. Whatever feeling you focus on and feed becomes stronger. You don't necessarily have to be right in the middle of a positive experience to feel positive emotions; you just need to engage your mind and decide to be happy and remember something that makes you smile.

Have you ever had a shared story or joke with a family member or best friend and every time you begin to talk about it around others you just can't control your laughter? Because many in the group didn't experience the same event you did, they might not get the humor in the story, but it doesn't really matter because you and your friend are both so into the memory you turn into dribbling idiots and end up needing a tissue to wipe away the tears of laughter.

This same idea can work at just about any time. Just decide to feel. You are already powerful and beautiful; you don't have to wait for something to happen to create those feelings. It's an amazing thing, but you can feel all those things with nothing changing in your life except your perspective.

If you want to feel like a giving person, give. If you want to be perceived as powerful, act powerfully. Not long ago, there was a young man who conducted an experiment. He hired a bunch of people to follow him through the streets of New York City with camera crews and act like an enthusiastic entourage. Thinking he must be a celebrity, complete strangers approached him on the street and began asking for his autograph. Viola, he was a star because he acted like a star.

Let your body lead the way to open your mind's focus on all the possibilities of achieving greater Emotional Intelligence. Redirect your focus and let it lead the way to create Emotional Intelligence. Instead of burying your feelings, celebrate them, use them to push you to maximum performance, more meaningful relationships, and greater satisfaction in life. If it's up to you to forge your own path, why not make it a positive experience by focusing on all that is right and good. It doesn't mean that you will never feel the negatives, but they won't be strong enough to take control of your destiny.

Just like you can use your positive feelings and emotions, you can also learn to use negative emotions when they arise. For example, if you are aware of your negative emotions and recognize their patterns, then use them to improve yourself. Like that knot in your stomach, we discussed earlier that happened whenever you sat down at your desk at work, use it to motivate you to get another job or change your career to one that is more pleasing.

It takes courage to make slaves of your negative emotions. Why? Because negatives can be strong motivators for change and change rarely happens without some struggle. Once you have a clear grasp on your feelings and understand how they can influence your life, you'll be willing to go through a time of discomfort to get to a better place. Suddenly, the tables will turn. Instead of being a slave to your negative emotions, you make them slaves to your actions and behaviors. Use them to push you to excellence.

First, you need to focus on the emotion, then on how you need to change your perspective, and lastly on your desired outcome. If you let the negative emotions control you, your focus will be limited and stifled. Remember, what you focus on becomes stronger, and everything you focus on is your choice. It's quite a freeing notion, this whole focus idea, wouldn't you say? If you want to wallow in self-pity, it's your choice. If you want to enjoy the positive feelings of a higher level of Emotional Intelligence, that's your choice as well. When you are exhausted, your inability to focus will be evident in the choices and decisions you make. To improve your focus, get lots of sleep. It's difficult to feel positive when you're getting only a few hours of interrupted sleep each night. Your mind becomes foggy, and you begin to question every decision.

Next, eat properly. If your body is the first to indicate your feelings, then make sure it's strong. Eat healthy food that feeds the mind and muscles. Avoid overeating and creating a sluggish system that can barely focus on getting out of bed in the morning. There are certain foods that fuel thought—eat more of those. I can tell you; they usually don't come prepackaged or in the form of frozen dinners or salty snacks.

Get plenty of exercise to burn off the unwanted negative emotions and encourage you to focus on a healthier lifestyle. It's much easier to feel positive emotions when you know you're looking your best. Exercise and healthy food create "feel good" reactions in the mind and body. Being physically fit released chemicals and endorphins that expand your thinking and encourage better focus and greater cognitive thought.

Whatever you do, do it now. Don't wait until you look better, feel better, have achieved more success in your job, or have found that one-in-a-million relationship. Remember, it's a decision, so decide now to focus on feeling positive and rejuvenated. Focus on where you want to be instead of where you are. Focus on what will happen when you achieve Emotional Intelligence.

Day 17:
Mental Health

Go ahead and take a mental health day from work. Everybody does it, even the big CEOs, though they'd have you believe that all they do is work 24/7. But you know what that is a recipe for? Burnout. And nobody wants to burn out, especially when they are a young professional just getting started. But there are some rules for when you go ahead and take this mental health day.

First and foremost, be honest about why you're taking the day. Tell your boss that you need to take care of your mental health because it is important for you to be able to function properly at work. Nobody can answer emails and phones and work on spreadsheets when their brain feels like it is on fire. Plus, honesty is always met with much more respect than when you lie about being 'sick'. Just tell your boss that you need a day to collect yourself and that you will be back in the office the next day, ready to conquer the world.

Do not send that email or text to your boss with your heart pounding in your throat. Be courageous. You deserve to have time to take care of yourself. This does not mean that you just leave for a week without telling everyone or that somehow you just can't ever make it into the office on a Monday. That is just taking advantage. Instead, every once in a while, it is perfectly understandable to just need a day to get the hell away.

Spend the day treating yourself, even if that just means sleeping the day away. How is this learning emotional intelligence? It is learning that every human has limits. When you learn to respect your own limits you learn to respect others'. Suddenly you stop making snide comments when one of your coworkers doesn't come into work. You understand when your secretary needs to go and take care of her sick kid. It just makes you a more empathetic person, which makes you a more emotionally intelligent person.

Day 18:
Look for Negative Emotional Patterns

There is a lot of negativity that happens in our world. People are upset because it is hard to pay off their bills, they have trouble at home, they aren't able to go on vacation or get a new promotion at work, and so much more. There are always things that you are able to be negative about, but if you fall into these traps, it is going to make it really hard to improve your emotional intelligence.

The first thing that you will need to focus on in order to get out of your negative emotional patterns is to learn what causes you to feel these negative emotions. Many times people will have stress and anxiety from working too much or worries at home, and this causes them to react with anger when little things don't go their way. Perhaps you are triggered when someone calls you a name because that is something you went through as a child. There are many different triggers that can make those emotions go all over the place.

The good news is that once you learn what these triggers are, you are able to get them under control. If stress is your biggest trigger, there are techniques that you can use to get the stress under control and if the stress does get bad at times, you can control your reaction better. No matter what kind of trigger you are dealing with, there are methods to help you control that so your emotions don't start going all over the place.

There are actually many emotional patterns that are easy for humans to fall into and which can make it hard to be in control over their emotions. This chapter will look at some of these emotional patterns so that you can escape them and gain the control that you are looking for.

If it is your insecurities that are causing issues, you may need to work on whatever is causing that in your life. Just because someone says something or constructively critiques you at work doesn't mean that you can just blow up and act in a violent or horrible way. Learning how to deal with these insecurities, or even what is causing those insecurities, can make a big difference in how you will react to others.

There are many triggers that can cause you to act out when your emotions are started. But you have to be the one who is in control of those emotions, no matter what. Learning what those triggers are and taking care of them as quickly as possible will ensure that you will be able to control your emotions instead of letting them take over your life.

When it comes to feeling emotions, most of us let the emotions take over and they get to be in control. When we are sad, we let the tears come and hope that others are going to feel bad for us, no matter where we are when they start. When we get angry, we let the anger and the violence come out to play. Often when the emotions come out like this, we end up doing things that we regret later on.

This is not how things have to be. You are the one who is in control of your emotions, you just need to realize this and start taking the control. Shifting your emotional state and choosing how you feel in each situation is going to help you to do this.

The next time that you are feeling angry and upset, stop for a moment and think about it. Is it really reasonable for you to feel this way right now? If you react, even if it is justified, will you feel happy with the results when you are done? What are some other ways that you can react or show your anger without harming anyone or being mean in any way?

Just asking a few questions about the emotion and seeing if it is even validated (is that person really that mad at you or being mean to you or are you just having a grumpy day?), can help you to see that the emotion is not really worth the way that you will feel later on. Yes, there are times when you are validated for feeling that way, but even during these times, you need to be the one in control, not your emotions.

Once you have a clear idea of the patterns as they stand, you can start doing your best to determine what should be changed first for the greatest overall result as well as those you want to double down on to ensure they keep happening the way they currently are for as long as possible. Changing personal patterns is easier said than done, however, as it involves changing personal habits as well, some of which may have been in place for an exceedingly long time. Planning is key at this juncture as it will be extremely easy for you to slip up and fall back into your old habits with really even thinking about it.

It is extremely important to follow through on altering the first few patterns that you notice for their negative influence as starting and failing to follow through on personal change is an extremely easy pattern to get into all on its own. If you ever hope to make real progress towards the change that you are aiming for then you need to make sure your pattern regarding change is positive rather than negative. Furthermore, you are going to want to keep in mind the fact that it takes more to make a new plan to change deeply ingrained patterns, it also takes commitment, plenty of time and a state of hyper vigilance that will prevent the pattern from showing up again when you least expect it.

Ideally, the best way to go about changing a specific pattern is to replace it whole cloth with another pattern that is going to fulfil a similar need in a more productive fashion. This new pattern will need to avoid all of the triggers for the old pattern so it may take a while for it to form properly before you get the hang of it. Regardless, it is important to keep it up and not use small instances of failure as an excuse for additional failures further down the line. Remember, it doesn't matter as much if you always stick to the new pattern right away, any variation from the previous pattern can be considered a victory.

It will typically take about a month for a new pattern to completely supplant the old one which means that minor instances of failure are to be expected as you get into the new swing of things. Nevertheless, it is vital that you don't use minor instances of failure as an excuse to revert even more thoroughly back to your old, negative habits. Sticking to the new pattern right away isn't the goal, that will come with time when you first start any deviation from the old pattern should be seen as a victory.

While you are taking stock of your common patterns, you are naturally going to want to flag those that are going to make it more difficult for you to continue making positive changes in the future. Additionally, you will want to be on the lookout for patterns that tend to demand instant gratification as they too will make it more difficult for you to make all the changes you need to make in order to be the master of assertiveness you can eventually be. Additionally, while the saying ignorance is bliss is true in some situations, this isn't one of them, make a habit of stamping out any patterns that promote ignorance ASAP.

Day 19:
Voluntary Action

Volunteering is one of the most important things a person can do. Volunteering is donating time, the most valuable thing that you have, to helping another person. Taking the time to volunteer somewhere is much more valuable than just donating money. Obviously, money helps because money buys things that help fill that shelter or help fill that donation box. But your time is also valuable.

When you take the time out of your day to go volunteer at a homeless shelter you are telling the people there that you recognize them. You were telling homeless people that you see their plight and that you were doing what you can to help. But most importantly, you're sending the message that these people are worth helping. Too often, the homeless are overlooked and written off as merely lazy or incompetent. When you take the time to actually go and meet these people, you are meeting them where they are at; you are recognizing their humanity. That can literally change someone's life. When someone goes for years at a time feeling like they are merely an afterthought to society and someone suddenly comes along and recognizes them as a human being, it can go a long way to helping them fight their way back and get on their feet again. Empathy, folks. It's powerful.

Volunteer at a homeless shelter for a weekend and actually make a point to talk to the people there. Make a friend – give a little extra to that person. Make them feel like a person, not just a cause. Because yes, it is important to advocate for a cause and to get things like homelessness taken care of, we have to remember that these are our brothers and sisters on the streets. So just make sure that when you volunteer, you take the time to make our brothers and sisters feel seen and loved.

Day 20:
Cleaning Out the Closet

I would like to close this book by talking about cleaning out your closet. This is an important step when making room in your life for more emotional intelligence. Being emotionally intelligent is recognizing that physical possessions mean almost nothing in this life. Being emotionally intelligent means that you recognize that when you make physical space in your life you're also making mental space in your life, which allows you then to make room in your life and in your heart for people.

This is not to say that material things are inherently evil. If you want to become more emotionally intelligent, you need to learn to let go to physical. You need to learn what matters most in this life are people and experiences, not things. When you clear out your closets, you are physically going through the motions of letting material things go and making room for more metaphysical things. You're making room for love, for empathy, for people.

Clear out your closets. Give away all of the things you don't wear to a shelter or to Goodwill. Don't take the receipt! Don't claim it on your taxes. If you claim your Goodwill donation on your taxes you are really missing the point here. The point is that you're letting these things go and no longer claiming them as your own. Learn to give for the joy of giving.

Day 21:
Setting the Right Goals for the Future

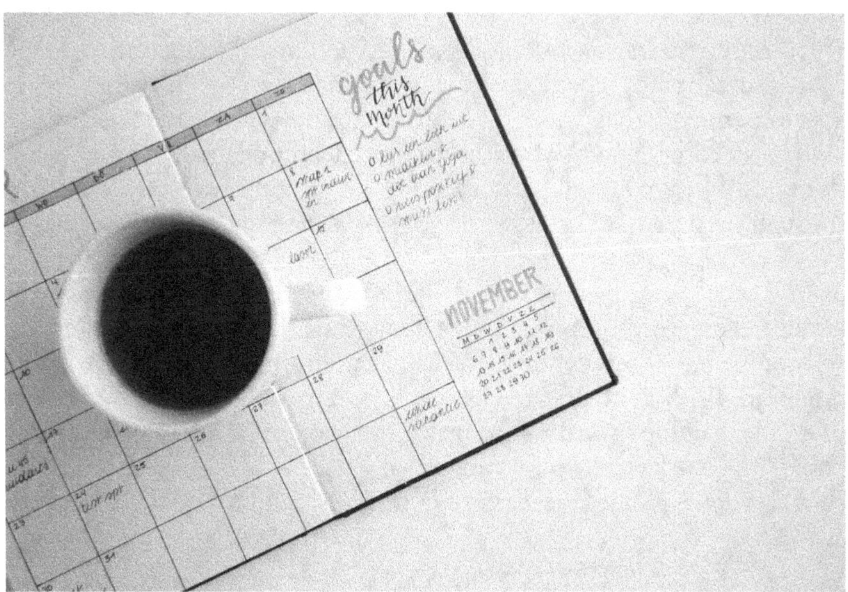

Improving your emotional intelligence isn't something that is going to happen overnight, it is far more of a marathon than a sprint. Thus, if you hope to see dramatic improvements in the long-term you will need to take small steps toward your goals every single day. One great way to ensure you stay on the straight and narrow is to ensure that the goals you choose are of the SMART variety.

Before setting a SMART goal, you need to have a general goal and for your first time it should be something that is both simple enough that you will almost certainly succeed so as to build the correct types of associations and neural pathways while at the same time being important enough that you can look back on it with a sense of accomplishment strong enough to encourage you to press forward when future tasks that are legitimately difficult arise.

Specific: It is important to always have a specific, clear goal in mind whenever you set out to accomplish something new. The foggier the goal, the easier it will be for your mind to come up with excuses to do something more immediately satisfying instead. Having something specific in mind instead gives you something to focus on when your mind starts putting forth excuses. Know your goal and focus on it when times get tough and you will find it easier to power through the right way.

If you aren't sure if your goal is specific enough, run through the 5Ws and H: who, what, where, why, when and how. If your goal is specific enough that you can determine who will be involved, what will be accomplished, where it will be accomplished, why you are doing it, when you will start working on it and how you will see it through then you are likely on the right track.

Measurable: A good goal is one where progress towards success can easily be measured, giving you a feeling of accomplishment and a serotonin boost every time you make another step in the right direction. With your first few goals, it is extremely important to keep them measurable in order to nurture the growth of the proper neural pathways. To determine the metric of success you should be using, start by determining the easiest criteria by which you can measure success.

This metric can either be one that is based on achieving certain predetermined outcomes or one that is based on cold, hard facts, the important thing is that there are clearly defined points that can be used to ensure you are always on the right track. Early goals tend to work better when the success metric is a number that can be easily defined as it helps to be able to constantly see a stream of new progress unfolding.

The best way to keep your goals measurable is to set up a generalized time table based on whatever it is that you have planned for yourself and then keep track of how you are doing in relation to it. This time table won't need to be extremely precise, as long as it has specific deadlines that you can always actively be working towards than it is doing its job. Keeping tabs on your success in chunks will ensure that you not only start off on the right foot but keep that success up all the way through to the finish line as well.

Attainable: SMART goals are attainable. When it comes to setting a useful long term goal, it is important that you choose one that is both far-fetched enough to be motivational while down to earth enough that it is actually possible. If the goal that you set ends up being too easily attainable, all you will have to do is think bigger down the line which is why it will behoove you to choose something that you can expect to ultimately come relatively close to achieving at the very least.

The trick here is to pick a goal that is attainable enough to keep you working diligently at it, while not so easy that it wouldn't make sense to have sub-goals surrounding completing it successfully. While 20 years out might be a bit excessive for your current needs, everyone can benefit from a good five-year plan. If you land on a goal that is either too difficult to achieve or too easy to warrant striving towards you will find it much for difficult to work to achieve it successfully.

Realistic: A good goal is one that is realistic in addition to being attainable which means that you can expect success without something extremely unlikely being required to push reality into your favor. A realistic goal is one that you are both able and willing to strive for in the current climate. It doesn't matter if you would be able to accomplish the goal if another set of circumstances were true, focus on the here and now and work from there. Realistic goals are also those that are set at a level where it will require work to reach them while at the same time not requiring too much work that they seem forever out of reach. Realistic goals that require a moderate amount of effort to achieve tend to create the most motivational force.

Timely: While you won't be able to tell a proper SMART goal apart from the rest by just looking at a few of its properties, you will always be able to identify one by its strict timetable including a firm start and finish date. Ultimately it will not matter how measurable, specific, relevant and attainable your goal is as without a firm timeframe for you to complete it in, the odds of it actually seeing completion drop below 20 percent. A good timeframe is one that requires you to put in real effort in order to see results, while at the same time not being so strict as to be completely unrealistic. Likewise, if your timeframe is too lax then it is unlikely you will ever put in the effort to reach it once and for all.

Conclusion

Thank you again for purchasing *Emotional Intelligence Mastery: A Practical 21-Day Guide to Improve Your Relationships, Increase Your EQ and Master Your Emotions.* I hope that this book provided you with the valuable tools you need to improve your emotional intelligence. And I hope you had some fun along the way! I certainly enjoyed writing this book and I hope that a lesson contained here that will inspire you to go on your own journey of obtaining more emotional intelligence. I hope you have learned that emotional intelligence is not something that is acquired instantaneously. I hope you appreciate that emotional intelligence is something that is gained after years of practice.

This 21-day guide is meant to give you a jump start. It is meant to inspire you to continue on this journey into using the tools that I have given you to continue to build your EQ. I very much hope that you understand that your EQ is just as important, if not more important than your IQ. Because when it comes to connecting with people, the first question on their mind is not going to be how many IQ points you have. Rather, they are going to wonder if you are going to be willing to understand them and communicate with them in a meaningful way. I think that I have outlined many ways in which you can start and continue to learn how to communicate with others in a meaningful way so that you can make them feel seen and heard. I also hope that I have given you the tools to help you better understand your own emotions so that when you are faced with a situation that requires you to reflect on what is happening, you can draw on your own emotional experience and respond accordingly.

I hope your butterfly wings begin hurricanes of kindness.

Other Books By Thomas Scofield

Discover 21 Powerful Techniques You Can Use To Build Self-Discipline And Achieve Your Goals Faster.

Do you want to become more productive? Do you want to learn how to achieve your goals faster? Have you ever looked at successful people in your life and asked what was their secret? If you said yes to any of these questions then you'll love this book.

One of the best ways to improve your productivity and achieve your goals is learning how to build self-discipline. When you know how to convert bad habits into productive ones it will be a lot easier to reach your goals and accomplish more in life.

However, becoming disciplined may be hard if you do it the wrong way. Avoiding temptations and procrastination everyday can't really be done without learning how to build powerful self-discipline habits.

In this book you'll find 21 proven techniques that will help you convert bad habits into good ones, skyrocket your productivity and achieve your goals faster than ever before. This isn't a book full of theoretical fluff. You'll learn practical techniques that you can actually put to use right away and that will help you accomplish things more easily thanks to the power of self-discipline.

In this book you'll discover:

- 21 Proven Techniques To Develop Powerful Self-Discipline Habits And Achieve Your Goals Faster
- The Right Way To Use Incentives To Become More Self Disciplined
- What Are The 2 Types Of Discipline And How They Can Improve Your Life
- How To Organize Your Life And Keep Things Simple
- Practical Tips To Sleep Enough And Still Have Time To Accomplish Your Goals
- How To Choose A Mentor To Help You Become Disciplined And Achieve What You Want In Life
- How To Better Manage Your Time To Be More Productive
- How To Teach Your Mind To Become Disciplined Using Physical Exercise
- Why Removing Temptations From Your Life Will Empower You
- 9 Affirmations You Can Use To Grow Into A More Disciplined Person
- Tips And Tricks To Get Your Diet On The Right Track
- When And How To Say "No" To People
- And Much, Much More

Learn how to become more disciplined and achieve your goals!

"How To Build Self Discipline" by Thomas Scofield is available at Amazon.